Animals on Mornington Island

By Coralie Thompson
Illustrated by Bindi Lee Day

I0163011

Library For All Ltd.

Wallaby

Goanna

Dugong

Turtle
(Barun)

9

Brown snake (Balangkal)

Curlew

13

14

Dingo

Crab

18

Fish

19

Brolga

You can use these questions to talk about this book with your family, friends and teachers.

What did you learn from this book?

Describe this book in one word. Funny? Scary? Colourful? Interesting?

How did this book make you feel when you finished reading it?

What was your favourite part of this book?

About the contributors

Coralie Thompson is from Mornington Island and belongs to the Lardil mob. She loves going camping and fishing. Her favourite childhood stories were those her parents told her about Country.

Bindi is a Noonuccal artist from Quandamooka country in South-East Queensland. Bindi's artistic journey has been marked by a modern style infused with storytelling that not only reflects her saltwater cultural roots but also pays homage to freshwater communities, forged through years of collaboration with traditional Aboriginal artists in central Australia.

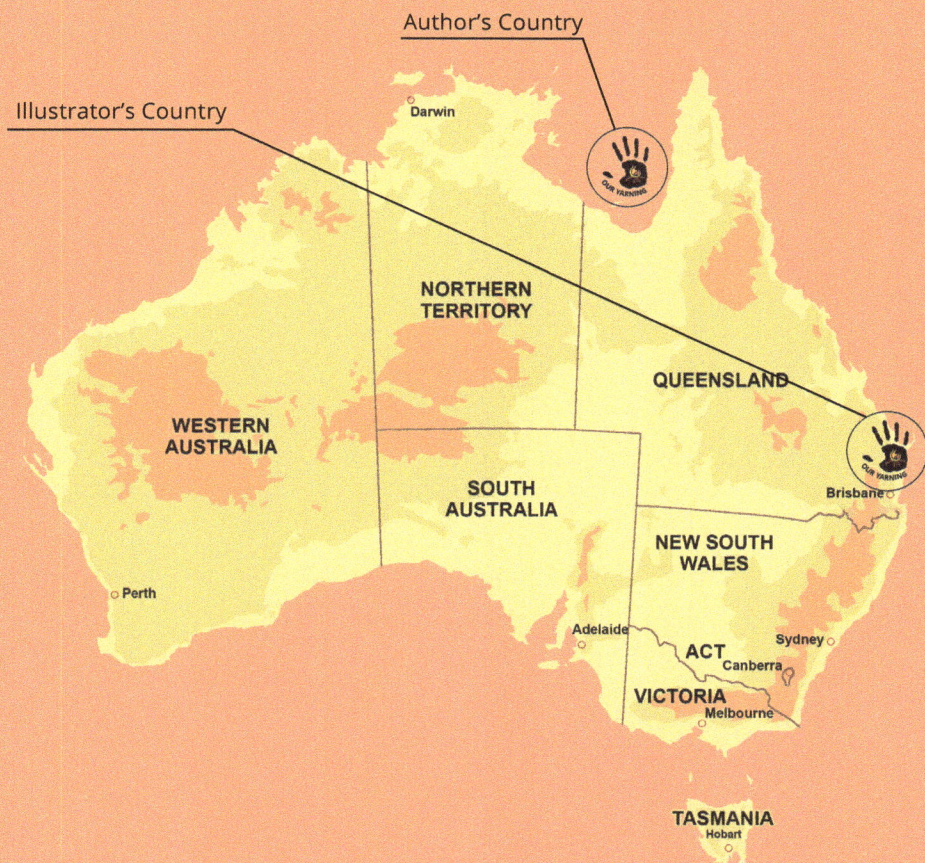

Author's Country

Illustrator's Country

Darwin

OUR YARNING

NORTHERN TERRITORY

QUEENSLAND

WESTERN AUSTRALIA

SOUTH AUSTRALIA

OUR YARNING

Brisbane

NEW SOUTH WALES

Perth

Adelaide

Sydney

ACT
Canberra

VICTORIA

Melbourne

TASMANIA
Hobart

Our Yarning

The Our Yarning collection aligns with the Australian Curriculum through the Cross-Curriculum Priorities — Aboriginal and Torres Strait Islander Histories and Cultures. The collection provides an authentic opportunity for learning and embedding Aboriginal and Torres Strait Islander perspectives because it is written by Aboriginal and Torres Strait Islander people.

We know that children learn better, and enjoy reading more, when they see themselves in the stories, characters and illustrations of the books they read.

To download the app, visit the Google Play Store or Apple Store and search 'Our Yarning'.

libraryforall.org

You're reading Learner

Learner – Beginner readers

Start your reading journey with short words, big ideas and plenty of pictures.

Level 1 – Rising readers

Raise your reading level with more words, simple sentences and exciting images.

Level 2 – Eager readers

Enjoy your reading time with familiar words, but complex sentences.

Level 3 – Progressing readers

Develop your reading skills with creative stories and some challenging vocabulary.

Level 4 – Fluent readers

Step up your reading skills with playful narratives, new words and fun facts.

Middle Primary – Curious readers

Discover your world through science and stories.

Upper Primary – Adventurous readers

Explore your world through science and stories.

Animals on Mornington Island

First published 2025

Published by Library For All Ltd
Email: info@libraryforall.org
URL: libraryforall.org

Our Yarning logo design by Jason Lee, Bidjipidji Art

Original illustrations by Bindi Lee Day

Animals on Mornington Island
Thompson, Coralie
ISBN: 978-1-923429-65-9
SKU04840

You're reading Learner

Learner – Beginner readers

Start your reading journey with short words, big ideas and plenty of pictures.

Level 1 – Rising readers

Raise your reading level with more words, simple sentences and exciting images.

Level 2 – Eager readers

Enjoy your reading time with familiar words, but complex sentences.

Level 3 – Progressing readers

Develop your reading skills with creative stories and some challenging vocabulary.

Level 4 – Fluent readers

Step up your reading skills with playful narratives, new words and fun facts.

Middle Primary – Curious readers

Discover your world through science and stories.

Upper Primary – Adventurous readers

Explore your world through science and stories.

Animals on Mornington Island

First published 2025

Published by Library For All Ltd
Email: info@libraryforall.org
URL: libraryforall.org

Our Yarning logo design by Jason Lee, Bidjipidji Art

Original illustrations by Bindi Lee Day

Animals on Mornington Island
Thompson, Coralie
ISBN: 978-1-923429-65-9
SKU04840